A COUNTRY HOUSE WITH SOUL

WHERE NATURE'S LESSONS UNFOLD

A COUNTRY HOUSE WITH SOUL

WHERE NATURE'S LESSONS UNFOLD

DAYLE GRANDE HERSTIK

Copyright © 2018 by Dayle Grande Herstik. All rights reserved. Printed in the United States of America. No part of this book may be used or reproduced in any manner whatsoever without written permission except in the case of brief quotations included in critical articles and reviews. For information, address Permissions@CitrinePublishing.com.

Editing and interior design by Penelope Love
Cover design by Rolf Busch

Library of Congress Cataloging-in-Publication Data

Herstik, Dayle Grande
A Country House with Soul:
Where Nature's Lessons Unfold
p. cm.
Paperback ISBN: 978-1-947708-03-7
Ebook ISBN: 978-1-947708-05-1
Library of Congress Control Number: 2017964534

10 9 8 7 6 5 4 3 2 1
First Edition, February 2018

Fort Lauderdale, Florida, U.S.A.
561.299.1150
Publisher@CitrinePublishing.com
www.CitrinePublishing.com

To the memory of my parents,
Ruth and Isidor Grande,
whose wisdom and foresight to build
a house in the woods provided
four generations of our family
with magical summers

To my husband Larry,
who always acknowledged
the true meaning
of this country house
and whose spirit encourages
the magic to continue

Table of Contents

Preface..*ix*
THE HOUSE: Beginning.........................*17*
THE PORCH: Creativity..........................*25*
THE KITCHEN: Observing.....................*35*
FIRES: Senses...*45*
THE HEMLOCK TREE: Solitude...........*57*
THE LILIES: Vitality.................................*67*
THE RIVER: Change................................*77*
THE ROAD: Balance................................*89*
CICADA SHELL: Shedding....................*101*
THE FOREST: Discovery.......................*111*
THE MOUNTAINS: Memories.............*119*
In a Nutshell..*129*
Acknowledgments....................................*135*
About the Author.....................................*139*

Preface

Wouldn't it be great if we each discovered a sacred place to rest into our authentic self?

This "authentic self" is not based on the expectations of others. It is not defined by our job, our function or role in life, or some unattainable vision of the person we think we are supposed to be. It thrives in noncompetitive environments. It is a composite of what makes each of us unique, how we see the world, our beliefs, our creativity and how we express our thoughts and feelings. It is the "core" of our being.

A Country House with Soul

Luckily life offers us a place of respite and rejuvenation where we are free to unwind, contemplate and see the deeper meaning of things. It could be a quiet beach, a small town we visit on a special vacation, or a destination we return to year after year.

I'll tell you about my place, a country cabin nestled in the woods of New York that has inspired me to share of its comfort and peace.

From infancy through my mid-teens, the summers at Casa Grande were an integral part of my life. Over the next few years, there were interruptions preventing summer time at the cabin. I grew up and my boyfriend, who later became my husband, spent weekends at the cabin with me and my family. With our being in the field of education, summers were free, or partially free.

My husband and I worked in summer

Preface

camps to provide recreation for our children. When camp ended we brought them to the cabin for about ten days, before school began. Eventually, after years of visiting, we no longer had to provide summer activities for kids—they grew up became independent and we began spending summers at Casa Grande. Of all the places I live and visit this is where I feel most peaceful. I, who must be busy, who must have an event to anticipate, who must have friends nearby, am in a place where none of this is readily available. Here, if I really desire it, I must seek it out.

I feel my parents' presence all around. I use the plates and pots they touched and sleep in the room in which they dreamed. My father taught me to swim in the river, though he was not a swimmer, and I can easily conjure up aromas of frying fish we caught there, and lamb chops. I remember the butcher sitting on the rocking chair, which is still there, writing orders for kosher meat with his stubby pencil. I remember the clicking of Mahjong tiles in the living room as I tried to fall asleep in the large iron bed with squeaky springs and a bumpy horse-hair mattress. I can still see my father going out at dusk to close the shutters, before windows were added to the screen openings. I recall the ten-hour trip in the packed, two-door green Plymouth, my father adhering to a snail's-pace speed limit, my siblings and I alternating in the front seat next to my mother, my head hanging out the window from car sickness and staying sick for another day. But even so, how I loved to come here. I still do.

Casa Grande means "big house" in Spanish. Grande happens to be my maiden name. It's not a big house. It's a cabin located in the Adirondack Park in Upstate New York, where

Preface

memories of my parents and the summers they provided live in the recesses of my mind.

In these pages, I invite you to experience solitude beneath the grand old hemlock tree with a glass of ice tea and a good book. Feel the lightness of being when you shed, for a while, the excesses of daily life in favor of simple pleasures like walking or biking on a country road. Join me in the forest and discover small thickets where unseen wildlife leave their mark, or see the mountain emerge from the early morning mist to herald a sunny day. Come to the river and relish the reflections in the calm waters or wet your hair on a hot day as you glide through the cool water. Spend some time on the porch, paint or be inspired by the river view and write a poem, or doze in the hammock. Pick some wildflowers for the table and enjoy a cacophony of color during breakfast with the lily garden in view.

A Country House with Soul

Eat a mouth-watering meal cooked over the open fire, then watch the waning embers of a campfire as night embraces you.

This book is about the natural environment in a contemplative place and how it has influenced my thinking. It's about my discovery of what I think is important, about how "less is more" and how little one needs to live a meaningful life.

A COUNTRY HOUSE WITH SOUL

WHERE NATURE'S LESSONS UNFOLD

· I ·

THE HOUSE

Beginning

"I've got a great place.
It's a country house."

—Lita Ford

My parents, Ruth and Isidor Grande, spent their honeymoon at a place called Scaroon Manor. Later on, after vacationing during two summers with teacher friends at a bungalow colony surrounded by mountains and close to a river, they built a cabin on the same road, overlooking the Schroon River. They called the house *Casa Grande* for the family name. It now serves the fourth generation of our family, mine and my siblings'. Almost everyone touches base here during the summer for the river, for the cookouts, for reading by the pot belly stove, for the air, for the unobstructed stars.

Everybody sleeps in the same rooms we and my parents slept in all those years ago. Groaning horse-hair mattresses on springs have been replaced, affording a good night's sleep. Two and a half bedrooms became four and a second bathroom helps accommodate a larger crowd. My parents' feather quilt is still available for cold August nights.

The kitchen faucets extending out of the wall and the green linoleum floors have been updated, though some of the pots and dishes are near ancient. The refrigerator with the ten-by-twelve-inch freezer has been replaced twice and now boasts a bottom freezer. The

The House

bench on the back porch where my siblings and I sat at the porcelain-topped table is now a table for twelve, built by my brother-in-law. Interesting mismatched chairs enhance its charm. The perfect, ice-cold drinking water comes from the well drilled thirty years ago. Thanks to my mother's foresight, it replaced weekly trips to the artesian well several miles away.

The living room furniture is of 1930s vintage. The twenty-first century is evidenced by the presence of wi-fi and a flat-screen TV. The old pot belly stove provides warmth and atmosphere for evening and rainy-day reading, though books are sometimes replaced by Kindles and iPads.

A hammock still hangs on one side of the porch ready to be hooked up for a swing. The age-old cot seems to be the most comfortable and sought-after mattress for the lucky kid who gets to sleep on it at night under a pile of blankets. What's inside the mattress is still a mystery but it is made attractive by a colorful throw and soft pillows inviting someone for an afternoon nap. The porch, overlooking the river and the great outdoors, is a place for writing and painting, and a blank canvas for small children at play.

During summer nights, the house embraces all inside. In the darkness, the sound of falling rain on the shingled roof, on hemlock branches and on small puddles is calming. A distant hum of traffic interrupts the cadence of nature's symphony in the dark.

We experience the bloom of early morning lilies, a thirsty hummingbird hovering near the hanging baskets, a golden butterfly alighting on a purple cone flower. We wait as the mist rises over the mountain revealing the sun in its glory, as sparkling lights dance

The House

on the river below. We take an early morning walk, talking about yesterday, a plan for today and the possibilities of tomorrow. Or, perhaps a bike ride brings us to a hill when arduous peddling promises a thrilling downward flight. We are renewed each day.

Home is an emotional state. Our country house is old enough to be a ruin. But it isn't. It has a history. It is imperfect, surrounded by perfection. It invites all who visit to become a part of this soulful perfection that permeates the environment. It is ideal.

Here in the cabin of my parents' young adulthood, we carry on the legacy that they provided for the family. It's an oasis. I see myself in my children, and theirs, as they explore, enjoy and drink in my summer world. There is no gift more precious than being part of a grand and glorious family tradition.

· 2 ·

THE PORCH

Creativity

"I like to sit on the front porch of an old cabin I built in the woods and listen to the birds."

—Johnny Cash

The porch is a good place any time of day. In the very early morning when the dew is still on the spiderwebs, birds are beginning to be heard, squirrels are scampering and the coffee is hot and fragrant. It's the time to watch the world awaken. Or in mid-morning, once some necessary chores are done, the phone has finished ringing and the road traffic is

A Country House with Soul

intermittent, it's a good time to write a letter. But the best time to be on the porch is in the evening, when the sun is gone and the mountain has darkened, before dusk. The quiet is pervasive, dinner is receiving finishing touches and maybe there's a bottle of wine on the table near the hammock.

Oh, the hammock! It's old and kind of saggy. A soft pillow enhances the contours fitted to a body and the table is close enough so my foot may gently kick it to achieve gentle swinging. Birds hop from branch to branch, deciding where to perch for the night. The leaves barely rustle. The mountain peak is clear. The river reflects the shoreline and the sky. I listen and watch. I observe nature as it comes to rest after a creative and fruitful day. This was a day when eggs hatched, fish spawned, pinecones fell and new growth poked through the earth. Lilies

The Porch

opened and are now closing, along with other blossoms that are short lived. Limbs of trees fell in the forest and small animals foraged for food. Spiders spun their gossamer webs and unfortunate insects became entwined, and bees buzzed and pollinated, ensuring new blooms for the future. Ongoing creativity in a natural form.

Here, surrounded by serenity, the porch is my studio, my reverie, my university. I can paint, or write, inspired and calmed by the river view. A hummingbird may flit near the feeder and drink. Vivaldi's "Four Seasons" may compete with distant noises, a logging truck, a whirring cyclist's wheels zipping by. All of this contributes to my creative self. My feeling of well-being. Yoga of the mind.

Standing before an easel takes concentration, commitment and courage. Why courage? Not everything turns out the way we

A Country House with Soul

envision it. We have to be prepared for small failures and disappointments, and we have to make changes until we get it right. Putting ideas and thoughts on paper is also a creative challenge. Hours and days can pass with nothing to show but crumpled paper or empty pages. Suddenly it happens and words flow like the river and there it is, a poem, an essay, a chapter.

Creativity is subjective and hard to define. It comes from within. It can be discovered, but it requires knowledge, experimentation, imagination and most of all desire. I have heard people say "I'm not creative. I can't draw a straight line, I can't even write a letter." Some have even said, "I spent my whole life learning and I don't want to learn anything new. I just want to do what I do."

I believe unlocking creativity is essential to personal growth, necessary throughout

The Porch

one's life. This creativity can be valuable to society, not necessarily the vast one at large, but your own personal microcosm of the society in which you yourself dwell, to give joy to others, as well as yourself.

How are we creative and fruitful? It often happens, when someone admires or comments on a work of art of some kind, the artist may offer small confessions of inadequacy. But everyone can create something and such caveats are unnecessary. There are many creative venues: cooking, rearranging, planting flowers, writing a short story about something you did, and now there's coloring for adults who insist they can do nothing creative, where colored pencils are employed to create colorful designs in a meditative way. When I paint, I sometimes have no idea what the finished product will be. After some struggling and plenty of redoing I am always amazed at my work. Or, nothing out of the ordinary has occurred—perhaps I heard a conversation or an idea popped into my head—and I begin to write a story or a poem.

Little children have no boundaries with crayons, clay or finger paints. Everything is a wonder. I love to spend time with my grandchildren as they get lost in the moments of painting flowers or dragons, molding clay bowls or a snowman, or making collages out of pieces of colored paper, buttons and cloth. They are so proud of their work, which went right on the refrigerator or on a shelf in their room. Each time they see it, it reminds them, albeit subliminally, of their ability to create something special.

I believe if someone renounces his or her creative ability, either the desire is not there, priorities infringe, there's no role model or

The Porch

they just don't take the time to sit down and create. We have to allow ourselves the luxury of setting aside things that can wait and take the time to let the music play, to let the visions come into focus as we write or paint something, or learn to knit or crochet, or do needlepoint. In the end we have something to show for our time on the porch of life.

Any time of day, either while sipping morning coffee, when the sun begins to rise over the mountain and nature slowly awakens, or when darkness begins to descend and the evening surrounds me with silence and cool air, the porch is a place for all things. Whoever finds a space here, be it a rocking chair, a hammock or an old cot dressed with a pillow and a handmade afghan, will find a view of the sky and treetops, spiderwebs and vacant nests in the eaves. The corner cluttered with brushes and paints, or the timeless table from the thirties with a surface used for wine glasses, books or writing material, will be part of a niche that suits the purpose of the moment and a desire to return to the porch.

· 3 ·

THE KITCHEN

Observing

"Know your food, know your farmer, know your kitchen."

—Joel Salater

Some think it's never a good time to be in the kitchen. Yet this particular kitchen is more than a place to find food and clean up after a meal. It provides memories, warmth and a variety of sustenance. It is not the same as it was sixty or more years ago when we were all young and didn't know about modern luxuries. We did have running water, a small refrigerator and an electric stove that usually worked. There was always food coming forth, far from gourmet but always enough to feed the family. Frozen foods were in abeyance and milk and cream were delivered to the bottom of the road. Other food came from the small grocery in town, or the local farm when the crops yielded beans, corn, beets and whatever else could be purchased for nickels and dimes.

Some of the original pots and utensils can be found on the shelves and are still in use. It was a place where my mother fried the fish caught in the river by my father and brother. The light came from the single bulb hanging from the ceiling and the studs were handy shelves for spices, napkins and whatever fit on them. The screen, which let in the light and the air, was shuttered when it was cold or rainy. One side of the shallow,

The Kitchen

heavy porcelain sink served as a drainboard and the two brass faucets came out of the wall. The water was either hot or cold; there was no regulating the temperature.

The countertop, which matched the green linoleum floor, provided a space for food preparation. The swinging towel rack was screwed into the wall and had three thin rods protruding for alternating use of thin dish towels, so there was always a dry one available. The cast-iron frying pans hung on the wall and the big pots that came from my grandmother's kitchen were in a cabinet that actually had a door. The fly paper hung in a long curl in two corners away from the food area. There were always flies on it and it was changed when deemed necessary. It was "rustic," or perhaps more "primitive" by today's standards.

There was always something to eat and

the water, which came from the spring, the only liquid kept on tap besides milk, was always very cold. Ice cubes were limited and rarely used. I can still see my mother standing near the sink, or stove, in her apron that went over her head, tied in the back, and had red flowers and food stains on it.

So many years have gone by. I look out of the window on to a field of ferns bathed in the half sunlight, half shadow of early morning. Beyond is the forest, slender trees reaching toward the sun revealing patches of blue. I recall my childhood, climbing the path and beginning my walk through the woods. Then there was a clearing and a tennis court for the occupants of this small community. It was decades ago, when the forest was not so dense.

The path to the woods is filled with a feeling of adventure. There are always sur-

The Kitchen

prises along the way. On occasion a deer or a squirrel pauses on paths leading in different directions amidst soft beds of pine needles, fallen logs to climb over, twigs cracking beneath my feet and plenty of blue sky.

The backdrop of the forest pines, birch, ash and others is strong and sturdy, seemingly protective of the waves of fern. An orange daylily emerges, to live its one-day life. Butterflies and small birds alight on the branches of the wild rose. A chipmunk scampers across a branch and disappears. What alights on our branches of our life? Is it something that we only sense or something that is heavy and burdensome? The strong and sturdy trunk is ourself and we need to protect the vulnerable branches that continue to grow outward as our lives progress.

Now I am at the sink. I begin to prepare a simple meal while listening to birds, and observing a hornets' nest beneath the eaves. Unfortunately for the spider, I open the window and the web disappears. Life is full of observations and so many things go unnoticed because we don't pay attention to small things. We miss so much. Here I observe another spider spinning a web and lying in wait at the edge. Small insects fly in, caught in the invisible web. But, the spider is waiting for the big prize and when it flies in, the spider will rush down and encase it in silk instinctively, making it its main meal. The small insects will be a mere snack.

Our daily webs are spun as we go about our lives in small movements. By the end of a day we will have collected thoughts, deeds and objects. We will have to decide on our main meal, a snack and what will be discarded. In other words, what is really important? How can we unclutter our thoughts so that

The Kitchen

we can concentrate on meaningful moments, to remind us of the beauty we have observed?

So, this kitchen, for me is not a place to avoid. It's a place to remember how things used to be. How it was when my mother wore her flowered apron. Children see things as they are. There is no extraneous knowledge for comparison. Do we see things as they are? Do we pay attention to our environment, the sounds, the aromas, the sensations? Do we see our loved ones as they are in spite of how they may appear? I feel I must pay attention to someone or some place or something, because it could well be the last time. By observing and really seeing, an imprint is left in our consciousness that we can conjure up at will.

· 4 ·

FIRES

Senses

"The echoes of beauty you've seen transpire
Resound through dying coals of the campfire."

—Ernest Hemingway

Eons ago the ability to control fire changed the lives of early humans. It was used for cooking, warmth, distress signals, the warding off of predators and for lighting the way. It also encouraged migration to cooler climates. When the hunting and gathering were done, it lengthened the day for social gatherings. Campfires are nothing new under the sun.

A Country House with Soul

At our cabin, fire is part of the overall experience, both indoors and outdoors. One is enjoyed on rainy days and chilly evenings. The other provides opportunities for cooking delectable hot meals and gathering together, stargazing above and flame-gazing below.

Our fire pit was created many years ago by our son, who visited after a camping trip. It is out in the open, away from hanging hemlock branches. As a matter of fact, all three of our sons have a fire pit in their yards, influenced by their experiences at the cabin, as kids and as parents themselves.

The campfire is a focal point at the end of the day when things slow down. Biking, swimming, hiking, gathering wild flowers, and tackling household chores are behind us. Preparation for the greatly anticipated meal has begun. Someone prepares the fire pit, then starts and attends to the fire. The

Fires

kindling has been gathered, by children if they are present, and the live branches for marshmallows are in abeyance.

The kitchen "staff" has been diligently preparing the food, which by the way is always decided upon at breakfast. Appetites increase and by the time the flames are reduced to glowing coals, the mouthwatering aromas of chicken, fish, hot dogs, burgers and corn make us ravenous. Everyone contributes so when the food is ready, so is the table. Two able-bodied people transfer the food to platters, carry it over and onto the side porch, and place it on the table that can accommodate up to twelve. It's the beginning of sharing bits and pieces of the day, with positive comments on the fare, hands practically intermingling as platters are passed around.

Wine, beer and pitchers of water from the well are plentiful. Any dogs present are relegated to the front porch, lest the tantalizing aromas find them begging to sit at the table. I see the mounds of glistening, freshly grilled meat dwindle as we all reach for seconds. At the end of the meal, leftovers are scarce and paper goods go right into the fire. Cold watermelon or other fruit is served. Some pitch in to clean up while others stoke the coals and revive the flames for a proper campfire. I love the bustle, the organized chaos, the sharing of time and toil, the mess we are all creating, which leads to the great reward of plain old good food. Nothing fancy, just delicious.

Someone has added some wood from the garage to awaken the coals. The kids have already gathered in anticipation of marshmallows and smores, roasting sticks at the ready. Parents begin to gather, bringing along the goodies and extra seating if necessary. There is some commotion until all is settled and the preparation of our second dessert is starting. The activity centers around the kids. A number of marshmallows wind up in the fire or on clothing, but anyone who desires has their share of the sugary, gooey delicacy. Twilight comes and we begin to be wrapped in a darkening cape. Parents do their best to achieve a hasty bedtime for hopefully exhausted children so they can enjoy what's left of evening.

Campfires have deeply mystical qualities. A replenished fire eventually burns to a comforting and mesmerizing glow. Verbal interchange ranges from sharing stories that conjure up memories to finding constellations, to deepening friendships and family relationships, to planning for tomorrow. I've never encountered an argument or harsh word around our campfires. We stay until the coals become embers and a feeling tells us it's

A Country House with Soul

time to go inside, perhaps for a cup of tea or a brief conversation before bidding a true farewell to what's left of the evening melding into the velvet night.

What does the campfire do for me? It awakens my senses. I remember the taste of the food. Gazing into a fire I find myself thinking about nothing. The crackling sounds are gentle on my auditory system, the aroma of burning ash or birch stirs other senses, and when returning to the now, I feel replenished and calm.

Obviously a campfire is not available under average circumstances. We need to find meaningful, everyday ways to awaken our senses, to calm the body and increase awareness of our surroundings. Notice how a campfire doesn't just happen. It requires planning. Energy is needed to gather kindling, prepare a proper "teepee" with dry wood

Fires

set up to keep the airflow going. Flames are needed to ensure the wood catches and it must be watched, carefully prodded, and respected. We are the same. We need planning, energy, and sometimes even prodding to accomplish and achieve our goals. We need mindfulness, and respect for ourselves and our life in order to keep it going, like the campfire.

When there are no visitors, my husband and I are the "kitchen staff." Food is basic and we do most things together. There is no campfire with all the accoutrements enjoyed after dinner in weather conducive to everything. As I mentioned before, fire is part of the overall experience at Casa Grande. On rainy days and chilly nights, we are not confined to a damp porch or cold living room that can be heated by a space heater that infringes upon the indoor environment of a country cabin. We have an old pot belly stove.

A Country House with Soul

Centuries ago, as you know, fire was the center of social gathering. Eventually family fires were created, and that became the hearth. After various modifications to improve the hearth by getting the smoke to go through pipes leading outside, chimneys were developed and they morphed into the pot belly stove. Since the time of Ben Franklin, these stoves were generally used in public spaces, such as train stations, one-room school houses and general stores. Here at the cabin, it's in the living room, the gathering place on cool evenings and rainy days. It's the only source of heat, so if one leaves the cozy comfort of the living room the heat will not follow.

When I and my siblings were small children, my father rose each morning, lit the kerosene stove for hot water, and then lit a fire in the pot belly stove. That's where we kids got dressed. In those days, before several

Fires

considerable renovations, the ceiling was very high. A lightbulb in the heavy beam was controlled by a long string, embellished with glass and wooden beads. A window beneath the front peak let in the morning sun, adding to the warmth we sought. Since those early days when the mighty hemlock was a sapling and the farmer who built the house rode past in his horse-driven wagon, the room was paneled and the light bulb was replaced by an overhead light and fan.

These days, after dinner my husband and I gravitate to the living room for the luxury of warmth provided by the pot belly stove. There we read, have tea, talk, or not. Rainy days duplicate these pleasant conditions and the crackling of the fire enhances the feeling of well-being. Within the room are some of the artifacts that have been ensconced in this inner sanctum since I can remember. We have the same furniture from the 1930s, redone when it became worn and frayed, and there are photos of my parents and me and my siblings as well as guests who made the long trek to Casa Grande by bus, train and sometimes by car. The bookcase my father built holds board games and magazines from the '60s and '70s, books about birds, flowers and wildlife in the Adirondack National Park, and classics, such as *The Deerslayer, The Last of the Mohicans* and several others. If not for that old bookcase, I would not have taken the opportunity to read these wonderful books.

The combination of sounds of the rain on the roof and the crackling fire awakens my senses and feeds my soul with peaceful feelings and fond memories, many of my father lighting the fire in the indomitable pot belly stove.

· 5 ·

THE HEMLOCK TREE

Solitude

"The best time to plant a tree was thirty years ago. The second best time is now."

—Congressional Record of 1969

The hemlock tree in front of the house is at least seventy years old. I recall when it was a sapling and had no function except to grow. Now in its regal state, it provides shelter for birds and their nests, branches for scampering squirrels and shade for us on a hot sunny day. This graceful evergreen grows on banks overlooking a river, in a forest or at its edge,

A Country House with Soul

but it is most impressive when it stands alone, its branches reaching outward, swaying in the breeze or at a standstill shading an area.

Historically, hemlock wood was not prized for construction, but used to make crates and railroad ties. The bark of felled trees was stacked and hauled to tanneries, where it was dried for at least a year, the tannin leached out and used to preserve and tan animal hides into leather. In the Adirondack area, the Pratt family had the largest tannery during the mid-nineteenth century. Unfortunately, due to a sap-sucking insect called the wooly adelgid, the hemlocks are victims of a blight.

There was a time when many trees were growing on the slope in front of the house leading toward the road. As they grew, they blocked the sun and the view of the river. Over the years my parents had them removed. Gone were the beech, the white pine, the

The Hemlock Tree

ash, the silver birch. The hemlock remained and flourished. This mighty tree that has been growing at the edge of the lawn of the house since my childhood represents stability, constancy, strength and solitude.

Beneath the hemlock tree is one of my favorite places to be. Sometimes I begin my day in the adirondack chair with a cup of coffee. I watch the mist rise from the river, birds flit, squirrels scutter. I see the bikers zip by. This is a place for solitude. Here I can experience the gentle sounds of natural things. It's not silence I'm after, it's the absence of noise. It is necessary to enjoy your own company if you want to enjoy solitude. It's different from loneliness. Loneliness happens to you; solitude is a choice.

We live in a fast-paced society. There are life changes—we relocate and leave familiar things behind, people die. Health issues may prevent us from doing some of the activities we always enjoyed. Then it becomes necessary to embrace solitude before it becomes loneliness. Loneliness gives a sense of isolation; solitude suggests a sense of peacefulness. It's desirable and constructive. It renews us to face the challenges of life. I'm not talking about sensory deprivation, but knowing how to keep ourselves mindfully occupied when we are not with others.

Sometimes, with young children and adolescents, there is a fear of being left out, forgotten or not invited to join, or being left alone at a party where almost everyone is a stranger. This can happen in adulthood as well. At a gathering others may be engaged in a conversation with someone, or in a small group, laughing, and for some reason you are not included. Perhaps you had a momentary distraction or you don't know everyone and

The Hemlock Tree

suddenly, a feeling of being alone, of being left out. Now you have to move around, get something to eat and then find someone to talk to. I have experienced this. I think that the fear of being alone is what propels one into a state of constant busy-ness. There has to be noise, music or television, which gives the illusion that we are not alone.

One can find solitude in different places: a special room, a park bench, a walk on the beach. Exercise, yoga and playing the piano are great solitary activities. These are opportunities to be in touch with yourself, so you can be in touch with others. So, I sit beneath the hemlock tree on a warm, breezeless day. I read a book, I write a letter, I doze. I reflect upon the moment and "get in touch with myself." Away from others I take time to sort things out, to decide upon priorities. I find my solitude to be inspiring.

A Country House with Soul

I might write my thoughts, my feelings, my memories, describe what I see, and sometimes it becomes a story, or a poem.

As human beings, we enjoy getting together with friends for dinner, card games, a cup of coffee. The company of others is necessary in order to appreciate solitude.

Yet a balance is important. Too much togetherness might lead to too much talk and extraneous noise and too little might lead to loneliness.

This hemlock tree has been a special place of striking this balance for so many years. My mother sat beneath it crocheting, listening to music through earphones, dozing. We sat, and still sit, by it with guests eating sandwiches, drinking cold beer or iced tea, always enjoying the view of the river. Years ago, when my parents were in charge, business was conducted beneath the hemlock.

The Hemlock Tree

They stood with contractors for renovations, reviewing prices, materials and time frames. The hemlock, evidently, is not only for solitude. It's a good place for discussion, heart-to-heart talks, to come up with new ideas and make decisions.

Very often it is a woman's instinctive role to be a caregiver. This is part of who I am. I cared for my children and my husband, my home, my mother. I kept everything in order, paid bills, made social engagements. Routines were intact; everything was like a well oiled machine. These were all purposeful and came naturally. Sometimes our actions may seem to just fill up time, but they are what maintains a family, a marriage, a life. Somewhere within the time we spend for the welfare of others, there has to be time alone on our own terms. This is solitude. Being alone helps to find the essence of self. Become a committee of one, for one person, yourself. Start with one hour a day.

The majestic hemlock tree is a symbol of strength, because of its stature and symmetry, because of its gracefulness and constancy, because it's been there since I can remember. It has provided me with shelter from the sun, and a lovely place for solitude.

· 6 ·

THE LILIES

Vitality

"A summer day sees the daylily open, rejoice in the sunshine, share its pollen with the insects, sense the day's end, and close.

—Susan Tyler Hitchcock
Gather Ye Wild Things

My father started the lily garden in an area boxed out by logs. One of the reasons for this placement was to prevent driving onto the septic tank area. Another was he did have a small garden in mind, one that could be seen from several areas of the cabin. It started with a few transplanted daylilies and after a few years, as lilies do, they multiplied.

A Country House with Soul

This was the beginning of our beautiful lily garden.

This perennial is a Hemerocallis, and not a true lily. It's a most desirable flower to grow, multiplying rapidly and providing a profusion of color. The flowers thrive in meadows, in clumps along a road and of course in border rows identifying the house.

Over the years, my husband and I discovered lily growers in the area and purchased reds, golds, and apricot-colored plants and added them to the garden. We separated and transplanted the blooms to other locations and they too became clusters of color. In the wild, they need no attention. In a garden they need space for the underground tubers to expand and for the bulbils along the stems of the propagated species to fall and take root. The tall stalks have many buds and each blossom blooms for only a day. Each day,

The Lilies

another opens and a clump of lilies provides color from June through July.

What are the qualities of a daylily that makes it so desirable? It is adaptable to soil and light conditions. It tolerates draught and has few pest and disease problems. It is suitable for all types of landscapes and a wide range of climates. It survives with little care.

So, as I examine the attributes of this sturdy, yet delicate bloom, how do I parallel my life, my thoughts, my demeanor? Some questions about lilies are: *How do you know which is right for your garden? Can it take hot sun? What is necessary to maintain its inherent character? Does it re-bloom after a while?*

The same can be asked of ourselves: *How do we know what's right for us? Can we "re-bloom" after some kind of emotional trauma, as we do after an illness or surgery?* I think we have to know ourselves and what makes us who we are. When it comes to situations in which we find ourselves, or relationships in which we are closely involved, how do we stay in them or extricate ourselves when necessary?

Can a relationship survive metaphorical desert-type heat or arctic winds? How much energy are we willing to expend to keep it going? Do we think it will re-bloom with loving care? It has been said it is necessary to eliminate toxic relationships from our lives. Friendships are one thing, family is another. Longtime friendships may fade or create emotional tribulations and the decision to end them is sometimes less difficult than we think. But when it comes to family, my belief is that you do everything possible to keep the relationship going. It doesn't have to be on a daily basis but differences must not lead to estrangement. We do not get to choose our family members, but

The Lilies

we do have choices when deciding who we want to be in our life.

The foliage of a lily should not influence our decision whether to plant it in the garden. The simple bloom, or the essence of the flower, is what will enhance the whole garden. Extraneous trappings and glib talkers are distractions and can interfere with a person's true worth in ways that mislead and disappoint. The same goes for those who appear unassuming, quiet and maybe are not so flashy in their dress—one of these can be someone you have been searching for. The lily teaches us to see past the obvious into what is compatible with our own values. Do we always see the foliage before the lily?

Lilies also have the ability to grow and multiply under good conditions without invading adjacent areas. However, a garden requires some barriers to achieve this. In the case of my father's original garden, he used logs from small felled trees. They have since been replaced with treated wood. *In our lives, what barriers are necessary to maintain relationships?* We cannot enter someone else's space unless invited. As the saying goes, "It's not what you say, it's the way that you say it." Tone of voice is essential in verbal exchange. I don't always recall exact words, but I can remember how I felt when something hurtful was said to me by someone I cared about. If they crossed the line into the inner space where I am free to bloom, it undermined the relationship. Sometimes it put a blight on it that took a while for redemption. Sometimes it ended it altogether. Perhaps I was a culprit as well, albeit not purposefully. Of course, perception and reality don't always jive.

Delicate they are, but lilies are astonishingly strong. The scape, or stem of the

The Lilies

daylily must be vigorous in order to support buds and flowers. Although there is only a single bloom, there are many buds that increase in size and weight that we want to reach radiant maturity. The flowers should not open all together and the scapes should be placed wide enough apart with room to expand and grow. The substance of a healthy and desirable daylily should not be so thin that it wilts before the end of the day. It should be as presentable in the evening, as it begins to close, as it was in the early morning sun, so that any hour of the day is a good time to see the lilies.

How can I apply this metaphor to my life? I will try. First, together with my husband, I have raised three children who are now adults with children of their own. They are not without their issues and travails, but who is? I too have gotten through a number of crises and losses, and in time managed to land on my feet. I have proven to myself, over the years, that I am resilient and I am still "blooming." We women, and men as well, should continue to grow, and not let all the "flowers bloom at once." It is important to find new interests, new people and new endeavors to keep us vital and continuing to grow and branch out. We must look for ways to revitalize our lives as we age so that we are interested in life, which will make us interesting to others, and presentable as the evening of life approaches.

So what are some special qualities of a daylily that make it unique and different from other lilies? It could be the color pattern, especially if it has been bred with other species. Or, perhaps it is the form and texture that is distinctive. Or, maybe it's just the wildness of it, growing just the way it was intended, free to sway in a breeze, attract a hummingbird, or just be.

· 7 ·

THE RIVER

Change

"What makes a river so restful to people is that it doesn't have any doubt, it is sure to get where it's going, and it doesn't want to go anywhere else."

—Hal Boyle

The river begins from melting snow high up in the mountains. Along its downward travel it collects rain and joins other streams until it reaches the bottom of the mountain and meets other waters. If you stand at the bank of the river, it is flowing deep beneath your feet unseen.

A Country House with Soul

The river is never idle. It has many moods. It is serene and sparkling in the morning sun, reflective of sky and clouds on a hot summer day, of shoreline logs and foliage painted by fall colors, or dark and raging in a storm carrying flotsam and plants to help nourish the life it harbors. It is a swimmer's dream in midsummer and a fisherman's reverie at dusk. It swells with heavy rain and rushing mountain streams, and once more changes to deep darkness and swift current. A cycle begins—the water subsides and once again it returns to serenity and visual clarity and a sandy bottom for your feet.

One day I was on the beach about twenty feet from the water and I noticed a small indentation. When I kicked it with my foot, it grew larger and turned inward. I took a stick and poked it and it grew larger and larger and soon there was a hole about ten inch-

The River

es in diameter, and then nothing. I stared in amazement. I dropped a large stone into the hole and in a few seconds I heard a noise. It was the rock hitting water. It was a terrifying and incredulous moment, for a sinkhole was forming on our beach, a dangerous situation. I covered it with a board and with the advice of the local EPA I requested a delivery of large gravel rocks and had it dumped down the hole. It took an enormous amount of these rocks to fill up this hole, which was probably twenty feet deep, or more. We were told that at one time a tree stood there and finally disintegrated after at least fifty years, when the area had been cleared. The river was flowing, as rivers do. This had to be addressed so its constant journey would continue without creating havoc in our lives.

I see the river from the porch. It inspires me to write. It calms me if I am agitated. It comforts me to know it's there, like a faithful friend. Sometimes I walk down to the river and sit there, remembering and visualizing the wonderful times we all had. I see my mother still swimming at the age of eighty-nine, her white swim cap touching the water. I stayed near with a large, smooth branch for her to grasp on her way back from her afternoon swim.

I see my children, young and as adults, on black inner tubes, floating in the sun. We all, at one time in our lives, deflated them just enough to fold them and sit astride, engaging in great water fights. I see my grandchildren, vigorous and spirited, glowing from the sun, building sand castles, carrying water in blue and red pails, or old pots from the kitchen to create moats and small streams for their fantasy worlds. We rowed up the river and explored the shoreline. We swam near the islands of

The River

stones and grass and ate jelly sandwiches in between finding pretty stones and driftwood. We all went to "Barry's Island," named by my sons when they were very young. They would hop in the rowboat and go up river in the early morning before we all stirred. It wasn't a good idea, was it! In those days we did things that today would be considered "not a good idea." But they looked out for each other as brothers do. The river was calm and low, life jackets bulky and necessary.

Many days, we filled two plastic quart milk jugs with sand, tied a long rope around them, and dropped them to the bottom. Attached was a yellow buoy, a souvenir from a Maine lobster barn. We secured a rubber raft to it and floated in the sun. If there were more of us, we added tubes, or another raft. We'd slide off into the water and swim. It was a deliriously joyous time.

A Country House with Soul

Today it's a different time and lives have changed. My children are adults, and so are theirs. Busy lives and distance prevent long vacations but everyone tries to visit for a long weekend just to be there. As soon as possible bathing suits are on and the river beckons.

My husband and I have taken many a solitary and gentle journey in the rowboat or canoe, up the river and around the bend, to Barry's Island. We removed bathing suits and swam, caressed by the water. Our intimate moments are still a source of magnificent memories. My grandchildren have come to love fishing with their grandfather, learning the art of baiting a hook, casting out, reeling in the fish, and the meaning of catch and release.

It has been said that "one cannot stand in the same river twice." Though it sometimes appears still, it is constantly moving, meeting

The River

with waterfalls, narrow streams, some dry areas with only trickles of moisture, and sometimes flowing freely around boulders and bends. When the river reaches its destination, it either mingles with other waters or becomes a stagnant pool, devoid of life forms. Such is life and all the encounters along the way.

Have you ever seen an '"eddy"? It looks like a small whirlpool staying in place as the river moves on. It appears to have a form and yet it doesn't hold the form, moment to moment. It keeps whirling. It looks like a "thing" yet it has no determining boundaries. Where does it end and the river begin?

There are times in our lives when our lives resemble these eddies—it seems things cannot get any better. Everyone is well. The kids are functioning and growing nicely. The world seems to be stable. Tornadoes, hurricanes, or other natural acts are simply not occurring

A Country House with Soul

"right now." But everything is a victim of impermanence and nothing is forever. The only thing that remains the same is change. Children grow up and leave to venture forth on their own journeys. Our careers are in the past, reversals of fortune occur, illness finds us, people die, love is lost. Change after change, the river continues to flow.

As I watch the ever-changing river I realize I, too, am changing. The momentary "me" is gone and has been replaced. I constantly try to grasp who I am, but that is futile, like trying to hold on to water in my hands. But it is not a bad thing. This ongoing change is my growth, my ability to see changes around me and adapt and accept. I learn to let go of things I don't need, things over which I have no control, small angers and, most importantly, disappointments. I try not to fear the future. I know the time I've had on this earth is far greater than the time I have left, a sobering realization. When one is twenty, or even fifty, thought is not given to the years ahead.

As for my husband and me, I know one of us will be alone one day and life will be different. I hope the wisdom I developed over the decades and stages of all my years will serve me well. And I hope, like the river, I will have the ability go around the boulders, negotiate the bends and avoid the eddies that remain in the same place.

· 8 ·

THE ROAD

Balance

> "Traveling the road will tell you more about the road than Google will tell you about the road."

—Amit Kilantri

The road beckons. Any time of day is a good time to walk on the road: morning, with cool shadows and a promise of heat and blue skies; or cloudless noon when the sun is high and the heat of the day is optimum; or evening, heralding the end of the day.

I walk, I run, I ride my bike and each type of lively movement provides a different feeling. Walking allows for thoughtfulness, running is more invigorating, and biking is like being lifted by the wind.

Where does a road lead? If it is straight I can see ahead, but if it begins to wind, I can't predict what lies around the bend. This road is familiar to me and so I know where it winds and where it does not. I'm aware of the surrounding trees, of the light filtering through the branches, reaching upward and outward. In July, the morning sun brings an abundance of wildflowers, clumps of daisies, profusions of golden black-eyed susans, yellow hens and chicks, swaying purple asters. The east side of the road abounds with poison ivy mixed in with innocent-looking creeping vines reaching toward and up the beech trees. Birds herald the coming day. Mailboxes, surrounded by lilies or asters or small rock gardens of red and purple blossoms, let me

The Road

know someone lives here, lovingly enhancing the environment. August blooms are scarce and some wildflowers linger, pretending that summer is not nearing an end.

Walking and nature are a perfect combination. It's like going on a small expedition where you find new and unexpected surprises, or, when walking on the same roads as I do, you are familiar with signs that tell you where you are and what's next. Anytime is a visual symphony on the road: early morning when the dew replenishes the flowers, late afternoon when the sun is low and nature's noises quiet down, or even later when the sun is setting and the sky becomes a palette of inks and grey. As we age, our desire to sit increases and we can find ourselves glued to a book or the computer or the TV to watch the news that is often not uplifting. We can counteract this state of stagnation by simply going for a walk.

A Country House with Soul

When we walk, we take ourselves away from the momentum of society and its constant distractions. The country road is a place to reflect on ourselves, to be in the present and to become rejuvenated by the environment. Here we are relaxed and unhurried, effortlessly absorbing the positive ions in the air. Walking briskly provides a different kind of well-being. It gets your heart rate up and your "juices flowing" and increases your appetite in anticipation of a delicious meal you later might be cooking over the open fire or relishing at the rustic restaurant with a lake view.

The asphalt is gentle beneath my feet and the silent steps taken feel like a small, slow-motion jounce. Ground garnet mixed in with asphalt glistens in the sun. An occasional car roars by, creating a delayed gust of wind, forcing me to the sandy shoulder, my steps crunching on the pine needles and pebbles.

The Road

If he's out, I wave to the local farmer as I pass his house where his ancient tractor and vintage car sit near the wood pile, ever increasing and always ready for chilly August nights and freezing winter days. I might stop and exchange greetings and learn another folk remedy for good health. That's where I learned about cider vinegar and honey in a glass of warm water to start the day. If he happens to be in his garden, I walk away with a cucumber.

Next I come to the diminutive cemetery. Several years ago, six graves were discovered. They are for the Pratt family, father and mother and four children. The dates are difficult to decipher, but they are from the mid-1800s. Resurrection of the stones and restoration of the small area was deemed a project for the local Boy Scout troop. The stones were placed in an upright position;

A Country House with Soul

the area, eight feet by five feet, was cleared and fenced in. Daylilies were planted and it's a small reminder that people lived near this road, across from the river, more than one hundred years ago.

A country road is not wilderness. It is wildness. Wilderness is untouched by hands or eyes. On this road there is a silent history of those who came before me, the wild ones who lived their days on the outskirts of the wilderness.

On the road, I walk vigorously or slowly depending on the purpose of the moment. I'm in a moving meditation, always aware of my surroundings. I can be by myself but it's also nice to walk with someone who takes my hand and loves what I love.

Sometimes I walk on the white line, one foot in front of the other. It's like walking on a balance bar minus the concentration

The Road

necessary to avoid falling. I am cognizant of my posture and I look straight ahead toward the winding road, alert to the sounds of approaching cars or bikers. I think about the importance of balance in life and how to achieve it. We must attend to necessary things that we may not like. But we must be sure to also attend to things we do like. We should learn something new each day, or do something we did before and perhaps do it better.

Walk on the straight and narrow and look ahead. Don't look back since that's not the direction in which you are going. Concentrate on the now. Breathe in the mountain air and feel the warmth of the morning sun, see the trees and the blue sky and feel an occasional breeze.

Free thoughts float into my mind, some fleeting, some staying longer. *Will it be a good day for a swim? What's for dinner, cooking in or out on the wood fire?* I think about my mother and how she crossed the road to the river. If I do turn around, it's only to pick the wildflowers for the table. Maybe I'll do a painting. I make a mental list of things that need attention. I remind myself to call a friend.

We balance our lives by learning, being productive and using our creative instincts. Cooking a meal, or even preparing simple food and placing it on an attractive plate, is productive. Researching the wildflowers, or looking up information about birds, is something new to learn. Take photographs, paint a picture, start a project—these will bring out the creative part of you. Write a letter. Write a poem. Within these categories of art, we will find some of the necessities for a well-balanced life.

Dwelling on things lost, out of reach or not within our power to change interferes with

The Road

our ability to move on. Sometimes "it is what it is" and we must try to weave it all into our life to make the best of everything. My children and grandchildren don't "live around the corner" so we don't see them as often as we'd like. There were missed opportunities to buy a certain house, to pursue a different job, to attend a family function that we should have. But we compensate and move on so we can be functional and happy in the present.

Life is a map of paths. We wind up somewhere unexpected and a new world is evident. Robert Frost wrote about "The Road Not Taken." There are more of those for us because we can only choose one and trust it is the right one.

· 9 ·

CICADA SHELL

Shedding

"I purge compulsively.
I'm constantly shedding things."

—Andrew Sullivan

This place that I inhabit for my summer respite is not like the big camps of the ultra rich, the steel, oil and railroad magnates of the late nineteenth and early twentieth centuries, nor is it like the summer cottages in Newport, Rhode Island, where the super rich and influential moguls reside. It's a cabin at the edge of the forest, built in 1935 by a farmer who happened to own a hundred acres of wooded land.

It's a simple structure built to last these eighty years. The basic accoutrements, such as furniture, porches, windows and pot belly stove, the internal structure as well as many kitchen items and tools remain intact. As time progressed, certain modifications were employed to keep up with the times and the needs of a growing family. Along the way items were discarded and replaced, usually by treasures found at garage sales or donations from family households. The house does have indoor plumbing and electricity. The kitchen is up to date with all appliances except a dishwasher. Some of the pots were touched by my mother, even my grandmother. The beds no longer squeak and there are windows over the screens, so no one has to go outside to close the shutters against the cold nights

Cicada Shell

or rainy days. There are the comforts of any home, albeit not exactly from modern times.

One day while walking outside the house in search of an empty bird's nest, I came upon the shell of a large, rather prehistoric-looking insect about one and a quarter inches long. It was camouflaged by the bark, shaded from the sun by a leafy branch. I used a large leaf to gently pry it from the bark, carried it back to the porch and placed it on the screened window sill. Upon examination I observed its perfection and how vulnerable it seemed. I supposed this shell was a fine protection against the elements and external intrusions. This hollow hull was the final stage of the process of a living creature's shedding the outer shell to allow for inner growth and expansion.

I wondered how many times this insect had shed its exterior membrane in order to grow. Other species shed their shell or outer skin. To become an adult, the cricket sheds its outer case, and snakes, no matter how small or large, leave their skin behind as they mature and grow larger, making room for their new selves. Lobsters molt as their flesh expands and sea otters replace their fur throughout the year. Children shed their baby teeth to make room for permanent teeth.

Shedding is simply a release of something cumbersome, perhaps of old ways that don't work, or things that don't fit or are unfixable or unnecessary. Shedding transpires when you discard something and give it to someone else who can use it.

The first thing I shed when I settle into life in the country are my city duds. I replace them with the clothes that got packed away at the end of the previous summer. Some fit, some don't. Sweatshirts and shorts, tee

Cicada Shell

shirts and flannel shirts that are decades old, and so comfortable. The number of pairs of shoes has been reduced to three, including sneakers. I don't think about what I have to wear. I'm shedding vanity. After examination, some clothing needs to be discarded, making room for other "new old things."

There is less of everything. There is one TV, less furniture. No window treatments to clean and adjust. Unread magazines and newspapers are not piled on the table. They go out pretty quickly, either to the pot belly stove to start a fire or to the transfer station for recycling. Mail is delivered daily and bills always find us. The calendar has few appointment notations. Locals who might be doing some work for us, dinner with friends, a film at the library, a concert at the performing arts center. There are local garage sales, art exhibits in nearby museums, and even dinners out. We don't live in a vacuum, we do what moves us. So, I have shed my frenetic schedule and look forward to being "in the day."

Since there's no dishwasher, the few utensils and plates used are cleaned immediately and put away. For a crowd, which is any number larger than two, paper plates are used. Cooking over the wood fire outside requires more work than a gas grill and somehow the food is more delectable. Used paper goods and leftover morsels go into the fire; then new wood is added for fireside sitting and stargazing. Phone calls are few and basic TV is for morning news or the weather, if at all. Here we shed the need for hundreds of channels to cloud our thinking and deliver more noise than we can endure.

The environment is conducive to simple pleasures like thinking clearly, reading quietly, blank calendar pages, few phone calls and just

Cicada Shell

being. I do have my personal amenities, such as my computer, my music and my paints, and I can attend to these amid calm and the aromas of pine or chimney smoke, depending on the weather and time of day. I come here to create, to write and paint, and to read. By the way, the sagging book case is replete with very old books, classics, like *Jane Eyre, Deer Slayer, The Last Of The Mohicans, The Bridge at San Luis Rey*, and many more. I have read them all, over the years, giving no thought to the *New York Times* Best Seller List.

What things weigh on us that are unnecessary? Is it the competitive spirit that might interfere with the enjoyment of just playing the game, or running at our own pace, or hiking a trail to see what we can see, not how fast we get there?

That great cliché "it's the journey, not the destination" never felt so true.

· 10 ·

THE FOREST

Discovery

"My home is in the woods.
My soul is in the forest."

—De Va

The forest is behind the house. It used to almost surround it but over the years, I should say decades, my mother had trees taken down to allow for light. I remember a time when there were enough trees in front to swing two hammocks, to partially obscure the road and to interfere with the river view. On the side of the cabin, stretching from tree to tree were the clotheslines where we hung beach towels and daily laundry my mother rinsed out in the tub.

Gradually these trees disappeared and to this day there are remnants of moss-covered stumps now surrounded by grass, natural growth and open areas for chipmunks to scamper and wild lilies to grow. There's a path behind the house and one does not have to go too far for a gentle climb to begin a walk in the forest.

As a child I used to walk with my father quite a distance because that's where we had a private "dump." It was long before the advent of recycling, transfer centers or trash pick up. It was the country, the land of solitude with limited amenities. So, once a week, my father gathered together the washed empty cans from vegetables, fruit cocktail, cranberry sauce, tomato sauce and whatever else came

The Forest

in cans, and we walked for about ten minutes to the area we designated for used receptacles, our private dump.

It was an adventure. I climbed over fallen trees, saw squirrels scutter, and looked up at the sunrays shining through the leaves, wondering how high the sky was and was God really up there watching. I searched for and found mushrooms, plants that survived without sunlight, and loamy ground formed by years of being undisturbed by human intrusion. I remember finding the skull from a small animal, the first I'd ever seen. I brought it home and kept it on the porch for years wondering about the animal and how it had lived in the forest.

The forest is never quite silent. As I walk about the trees now, I hear sounds of twigs crunching, branches snapping, a bird calling. I observe my surroundings and soon discover unexpected treasures. I used to think that brown is, well, brown. Here in the forest there are so many browns: umber, teak, mahogany, almond. Green was green, but now I see colors varying from yellows to the pale green of a new fern to the deep blue-green of spruce. When I stop to ponder in a thicket, I gently move pine needles and discover red toadstools, fallen nuts and wild berries. I use a branch to push away leafy boughs so I can follow a path and suddenly there's a deer about twenty feet away. I come across small caves, which are protection for small animals. Here and there are bowl-shaped plants, collecting water. I quietly observe as I carefully walk, not on a path, but in a familiar direction. Beetles, small frogs and the mighty ant carrying one-hundred times its weight continue their activity.

My discovery of nature's wonders fills

The Forest

me with awe and surprise. Who knew there was a stream that curved around a bend and flowed downward toward the river after the rain? How did that natural bench get there, providing a place to sit and watch and listen, and breathe in the sweet aromas of the forest? A place to rest beneath the light filtering through the canopy of trees, the oaks, the silver birch, the beech, the tall pines, some so thin because of the lack of intense light.

Time in the forest is measured by cycles of light and darkness. Much has happened to change the forest just as much has happened to me in my life cycle, as I grew from a small child to where I am in my life now. The forest will continue on and change with new growth and new wonders. It is necessary for us to continue to grow as we get older—to change our perspective so we can see the world differently and open ourselves up to new ideas. To take a different path for who knows what we will discover along the way. A new friend, another street, different ideas from another culture. I know that I continue to grow and change, evidenced by what I learn by my self-discovery, which is so clear when I walk in the forest.

· II ·

THE MOUNTAINS

Memories

"Mountains have their own memories. All the old memories rooted in the earth."

—Christopher Scotton
The Secret Wisdom of the Earth

The farmer and his sons built the cabin with their own hands using tools of the time. They raised the simple, sturdy structure on the west side of the mountain, on the hill where the river can be seen as it gently flows, rages swiftly or sparkles in the morning light.

The dark mountain is brushed with a green glow at sunrise. As I look toward the east, I can make out the marker, the huge bald spot, the great rock where climbers rested and observed the world. The great tall pines are not individualized; they coat the mountain with a fluffy surface that belies the height of the towering trees. The mist rises over the river only to dissolve in the air as it kisses the shoreline. The sunrise is soon complete. The trees glisten and some of the trees stand out like the random cluster of birch, their trunks and branches gleaming silver in the morning sun. The mountain, bathed in sunlight, nourished by rain, painted by autumn or blanketed in snow, is majestic and loyal, always there to absorb time and enjoy its own memories.

I remember one summer day when we crossed the valley road and walked down to the river, a group of eight adults and eight kids. We piled into rowboats, crossed the river,

The Mountains

tied up the boats, grabbed our own gear and began our journey. I was ten years old.

We walked through the field of milkweed, daisies and clumps of grass, where butterflies flitted, grasshoppers jumped and crickets chirped. Long pants, long sleeves and good shoes protected us from insects, brambles and branches. We arrived at the base of the mountain, at the path known from previous climbs, and started our walk up the gentle slope of the mountain. We climbed over boulders and stepped into streams, hearing birdcalls and chipmunk chatter. We didn't give a single thought to snakes. Unaware that we were climbing on a diagonal, adults interspersed with children, we came to a clearing surrounded by wild blueberry bushes, lit up by sunshine and blue sky. Our work began as we picked small clumps of juicy berries and let them fall into the two giant-size tomato juice cans dangling from strings around our necks. The adults chattered and laughed and told little stories while we kids were very serious about filling up the cans, which would have happened more quickly if we hadn't eaten more than we picked.

We moved on to other clearings and soon it was time to stop and eat our lunch. We had arrived at the bald spot, the huge rock, open to the sun, where we sat and ate cheese sandwiches, drank water that had been frozen in a milk carton, perfect for thirst quenching, and treated ourselves to more fresh wild blueberries. We all stood together and waved shirts and yelled, "HELLO!! WE'RE HERE!!" We couldn't see any people down at the bottom of the world, and we'd find out later that they all, indeed, saw us.

When watches indicated it was twelve

The Mountains

noon, we knew we'd been out for three hours. The downward trek was faster and easier, although we were painfully aware of the full cans around our necks. We arrived at our destination in the heat of the day. The swimmers greeted us with gusto. Rowing back across the river seemed to take forever. We jumped out, placed all the cans in a safe area, and, prepared with bathing suits, removed our top layers of clothes, and jumped into the river. It was a glorious time.

What a bounty we had! All those juicy, sweet blueberries! There would be blueberry pancakes, blueberry pies, and blueberries and cream.

What do such memories mean to us? How do we conjure them up and what keepsakes do we have to remind us of times of wonder, times of strife? Photos, autograph albums, dishes, cookware, clothing, baby toys and clothes, report cards, drawings, diaries. Do we discard all things deemed useless or outdated? Or do we hold on to them as keepsakes of our memories?

Recently I discovered a well-preserved shoebox in a closet. It was filled with cards, letters, menus. They were letters I'd written to my parents, birthday cards signed by people I remember, long gone. As I perused and read them, my memory was jolted and I could recall so many things, so many faces I hadn't thought of in years. Among this treasure trove were telegrams honoring my parents wedding day, my birth, my brother's Bar Mitzvah. My granddaughter had never heard of a telegram, much less seen one. Delightedly she took them and framed them behind glass and they hang on a wall in her home, near photos of her grandparents and her parents as children.

The Mountains

When I use something my mother or grandmother touched, it truly gives me pause, just remembering who came before me. Just think! Four generations have spent time in this house. I'm warmed by the thoughts that my granddaughter finds these things of interest and importance and that she, too, will know her own heritage.

At any time of day or evening, I see the mountain in its majesty and know it overlooks the world I knew as a child. Yes, the mountain remembers.

· 12 ·

IN A
NUTSHELL

When I ask my grandchildren,
"Where do you like to visit best?"
they all say, "the country house."

—Dayle Grande Herstik

The narrative you have read is based on at least seventy years of vivid memories. Looking back on those years has been significant and meaningful for me. I was able to conjure up feelings, aromas and tastes that played an important part in my life. I translated those sensations and reactions into my present philosophy of life.

A Country House with Soul

For starters, it's essential to have empty space. Space in a room, so there are uncluttered places to rest your eyes. Space on a calendar, to make dates for a necessity or enjoy a spontaneous event. Space to stretch out ourselves and feel unencumbered by objects or people. Our lives are cluttered with important things as well as trivia. When we find ourselves in a place that is open and bright, with pleasing scents, we have space to increase our capacity for simply being. We need to take the time to accomplish this by creating this kind of space for ourselves in a room or even in a corner of a room. All you need is a bright area with simple items of comfort, pleasing to the eye, and a window.

The space depicted in this book is vast. It is spread out among the trees and a great open sky, interrupted only by nature's patterns of mountain peaks. Here my eyes can dwell on

In a Nutshell

the lilies, the hemlocks or even the mailbox at the bottom of the road, and of course, the river. Nothing appears crowded, allowing for things of beauty to be individually significant. For the spiritual well-being of our family, my husband and I try to keep it that way, and when trees or other foliage needs trimming, we know who to call.

Of course, things need to be repaired and replaced. The house needs heavy cleaning upon opening to prepare for summer living and again on closing in anticipation of a harsh winter. Don't be misled: maintenance, money and time are all necessary to be in a place like this. Leading a simple life can be hard work.

Here at Casa Grande there is time to be quiet. My beloved and I can be by the river, or by the pot belly stove fire, and read and not talk, if we desire. Sometimes there is music to keep us company. We comment on the news, on a passage from a book. We are always communicating. We talk while eating, while enjoying a glass of wine, during kitchen clean up. Things rev up when family or friends visit. There's ongoing conversation, planning, philosophizing and of course young children are always doing something that requires animation and verbal exchange. Yet, everyone manages to take time to find a quiet place for solitude, reading, dozing, and doing crossword puzzles, as they please.

All the while, the river sparkles, rushes or meanders. Early morning birds flit through trees, squirrels scamper. Heavy clouds bring rain, nourishing the earth, tamping down the dust. The dusk turns into night, and the constellations appear across the darkness. There is continuity, there always has been. Life is just a matter of taking the time to understand and appreciate it.

Acknowledgments

Thank you to my editor, manager, publisher and literary colleague, Penelope Love of Citrine Publishing, for your guidance, our face-to-face meetings and your gentle revisions, which always made sense.

Thanks with love to my husband, Larry, for our discussions and his helpful insights that reinforced the beauty of the surroundings at the heart of this book, and for keeping the beach in perfect condition. I wish you had seen the finished product. You'd have loved it.

A Country House with Soul

Thanks to my sister, Helene Epstein, who shared our timeless summers of childhood and beyond, as well as to her husband, Albert, who always brought his tool box and expertise in all things needing repair.

Thanks to my brother, Paul Grande, for his invaluable business sense as well as his ability to understand the best ways to do things, and to his wife, Nance, whose recipes were always a hit.

I would be remiss if I didn't mention all the children: Neal, Ivan and Barry Herstik, Laurie and Jonathan Epstein, and Allan, Sara and Ian Grande, whose visits revitalized the lives of their grandparents, and their children who enhanced the lives of their grandparents and great grandmother, and who continue to bring joy to this special place as well as help maintain the house with new ideas and vitality.

Acknowledgments

Finally, I would like to acknowledge the National League of American Pen Women for surrounding me with erudite women who inspire me to continue creating.

About the Author

Dayle Grande Herstik is the author of the *When We Were Perfect: A Book of Poetry*, *Life Happens: A Collection of Short Stories*, and *A Country House with Soul: Where Nature's Lessons Unfold*, wherein life's wisdom and tiny moments linger upon the landscape of her family's Upstate New York summer country home. The common threads of her books and writings are her experiences, relationships and philosophy.

A Country House with Soul

In her eyes, growing up in Brooklyn, New York, in the '50s offered the best of everything. That was the true Age of Innocence. The neighborhood provided friendship and a sense of unity. To this day, she has close ties with her childhood friends. They share memories and the special bond of people with whom there is a history and who "knew you when."

Dayle met her husband, Larry, while attending Brooklyn College. After the early days of marriage and three children, she furthered her education and followed a career as a teacher of speech improvement, and then as a supervisor and administrator for the New York City Public Schools. She was also in private practice providing speech therapy for young children.

In "retirement," her time is divided between Boca Raton, Florida, New Jersey,

About the Autor

and the Adirondack Mountains in New York State. She is a member of the National League of American Pen Women.

Ms. Herstik may be contacted through the publisher.

Dear Reader,

Thank you for reading. If you enjoyed this book, kindly support the author's efforts by helping others find it. For instance, if you would like, you could:

 * Write an online customer review.

 * Gift a copy of this book to a friend.

 * Suggest this book to your local book club.

For orders of ten books or more, please contact Citrine Publishing at (561) 299-1150 or email Publisher@CitrinePublishing.com.

Thank you again! We cannot begin to tell you how important your feedback is to us.

> *Sincerely,*
> *Penelope Love, Publisher*

www.ingramcontent.com/pod-product-compliance
Lightning Source LLC
Chambersburg PA
CBHW021440080526
44588CB00009B/624